HOW TO REMEMBER NAMES

HOW TO REMEMBER NAMES

Dr. Thomas Crook
with Christine Allison

A JOHN BOSWELL ASSOCIATES BOOK

HarperCollins*Publishers*

FIRST EDITION

Designed by Helene Berinsky

Library of Congress Cataloging-in-Publication Data
Crook, Thomas.
  How to remember names / by Thomas Crook with Christine Allison.—1st ed.
    p.   cm.
  ISBN 0-06-016628-2
  1. Mnemonics.   2. Names, Personal.   I. Allison, Christine.   II. Title.
BF387.N34C76   1992
153.1′4—dc20   91-50457

92 93 94 95 96 DT/RRD 10 9 8 7 6 5 4 3 2 1

Contents

Acknowledgments

No one did more to move this book to its completion than Anastasia Zadeik-Hipkins. Stacy took our complex and voluminous research and distilled it into something readable and friendly. Her caring and professionalism are reflected in this book, from cover to cover.

I would also like to thank our editor, Craig Nelson, for understanding, as we do, that there are thousands of people in need of practical memory advice. From the start he shared our objective—to produce the best book possible—and I am immensely grateful.

—TC

HOW TO REMEMBER NAMES

Introduction:

"MR. BURPEE, I PRESUME?"

The legendary Clare Boothe Luce was once sitting next to David Burpee, chairman of Burpee & Co., the seed company, at a small dinner party. The quintessential gentleman, Burpee became aware halfway through the evening that Mrs. Luce had forgotten his name, and he sought to put her at ease.

He leaned over to her and whispered, "I'm Burpee." Mrs. Luce looked at him blankly and then recovered, patting his hand. "That's all right," she said reassuringly, "I get that way sometimes myself."

No one is immune from the embarrassment of a forgotten name. Yet if there is one skill that gives you the advantage in business and personal relations, it is the ability to remember people's names. Dale Carnegie identified name recall as *the first fundamental of effective people relations*. "There is no sound sweeter than a person's own name," he writes in his best-selling book *How to Win Friends and Influence People*. A remembered name is often the ticket to a friendship, a closed deal, or a new partnership, and it generates instant goodwill in a way no other courtesy can.

In 1985 I founded Memory Assessment Clinics, Inc., after I had spent more than fourteen years studying memory as a clinical psychologist at the National Institute of Mental Health. My goal was to form a team of experts who would develop new tests to assess memory abilities and new ways to improve memory. Since then, our team has analyzed the memory abilities of more than ten thousand individuals all over the world and tested many new treatments for memory disorders. From Finland to Japan, the number one complaint we have heard—in all cultures—is "I just can't remember people's names." We have worked with men and women at the highest levels of their professions—the famous and the not-so-famous—in an effort to understand memory, improve memory skills, and remove psychological obstacles to a powerful, active memory.

There is little question that a failing or uneven memory can deflate self-esteem, interfere with the ability to function in the most common everyday activities, and take its toll on business effectiveness. When it comes to forgetting people's names, an unreliable memory can hurt feelings and create negative impressions that can be very difficult to reverse.

But it doesn't have to be that way. Our team of specialists has refined and clarified the best memory training techniques and made them simple to grasp and easy to use. I suppose that if there is one thing that distinguishes our work in this field, it is the conviction that real-life considerations are what matter most when it comes to the human memory. I am not a believer in people memorizing arcane information just to show off at parties; I'm more interested in helping people remember the name of someone they just met, what they read in a newspaper or magazine, or instructions they are given to complete an important task.

What I am after, in a word, is memory that is *useful*.

WHY YOU SHOULD EVEN CARE

When we forget a person's name, especially in an important business or social situation, it can be disturbing. We feel socially inept, uncomfortable, and embarrassed, and we may have made an extremely bad first impression. While this might not be the worst thing in the world, if you're in business, it can have serious consequences.

My friend John, whose wife is a prominent attorney, told me that one of his wife's new employees—a reputed whiz—called her frequently at home in the evening. The frequent calls were no problem, but the young man's manners were. Every time my friend answered the phone, there would be an awkward pause, clearly because the young man was stumped for John's name.

"I know I was being overly sensitive," John said, "but after three or four episodes, it became so insulting that I started making rude remarks about this fellow to my wife. There were other problems with him, and eventually he was fired. But let's face it: husbands and wives influence each other, whether they admit it or not. I've always felt a little guilty about my role in his getting the ax."

In a broader sense, I have often found among people in business that the failure to take the time and effort to remember people's names is symptomatic of the inability to relate to people in general.

An example that comes to mind is an experience I once had serving as a consultant to a large company considering which of three senior executives would be elevated to the rank of president. Rather than interview them in an isolated office environment, I asked to spend several hours with each candidate during the course of a normal working day.

I remember being surprised that one of the three men, in clear contrast to the other two, appeared to know the names of very few employees under his supervision. As we toured a production area he continuously responded to workers with vague and nameless greetings, such as "How's it going?" or by substituting "son" or "kiddo" for the name. I could not help but note this in my report since the job of company president involved considerable social interaction with a broad range of people. The job ultimately went to one of the other candidates.

What intrigued me, however, was that wholly apart from my assessment, the candidate who had taken neither the time nor the energy to remember his employees' names was ranked by those same employees far below the other two candidates. His ratings for technical proficiency and production knowledge were excellent, but his interpersonal skills were so poor it may have cost him a crucial promotion. If this man had simply taken the time and exerted the effort to remember the names of his employees, he might well be president of his company today.

While the costs of not knowing someone's name can be high, the rewards of remembering a name can be immense. Remembering someone's name produces an *enduring, positive first impression.* In receiving lines at state dinners at the White House, it is proper protocol for an aide to whisper the name of the next person in line to the President of the United States. Most of the people in line realize that the President does not recognize them personally, but the impact of this courtesy is profound.

We implicitly trust someone who remembers who we are. And while the conscious impression of remembering someone's name is short-term, the subconscious impression is lasting.

An acquaintance who is a restaurateur in New York City makes a point of remembering people's names. One evening one of his regular customers brought a friend into his restaurant and introduced her as Connie. The restaurateur gave the twosome a perfunctory hello and welcome. Two hours later, as they were leaving the restaurant, he said, "It was really nice meeting you, Connie."

"From the look on her face—which was one of both shock and enormous pleasure—I could tell not only that she would be back again, but that she would probably bring in new customers," the restaurateur told me. "So much of the restaurant business is word-of-mouth. Remembering one person's name is the kind of thing that can get you a hundred new patrons."

In the chapters that follow, you will not only learn the strategies you need for remembering people's names but also find that in using these strategies your memory as a whole will become crisper, faster, and more responsive. You will find yourself paying better attention, whether it is to a face, the front page of the newspaper, or the next move in your bridge game.

You will also learn strategies that address other aspects of your daily life. Though remembering people's names is by far the most frustrating memory task, there is a long list of secondary concerns, such as remembering phone numbers, shopping lists, where you put your keys . . . and those glasses that always seem to "disappear." In the final chapter of the book, you will find dozens of quick, easy-to-use exercises that will improve your memory on all of these fronts.

Getting a handle on your memory is taking control of your life in the most fundamental way. After all, your memories of past experiences establish who you are, and if your memory is not serving you well, your ability to function successfully will be greatly diminished.

Over the past twenty years, I have studied many conditions associated with memory loss, including Alzheimer's disease. In this disorder, individuals and their families suffer on a scale that most of us cannot imagine. Victims of Alzheimer's disease and their families have little control over the pathological destruction caused by the disorder. But most people have the ability to preserve their intellectual and memory abilities throughout life, and thus keep their minds exercised and fit. This is what memory training is all about.

I do not, however, believe that something that is good for you must necessarily be tedious, repetitive, or overly complicated. Getting your memory into shape will take a little work—there are no elixirs or magic words that can sharpen your mind—but I think you will find the exercises in this book almost painless and maybe even entertaining. The book is as short as we could make it; your commitment need only be the time it takes you to go through it. But if you are willing to make that commitment and really focus on the contents, you will see marked improvement in your memory abilities.

In fact, our research has shown that the techniques you will find in this book can boost your recall by 40 percent—or more.

1

How We Remember

Even a baby knows the importance of remembering people's names. I'd wager that your first word was a person's name—and that when you miraculously came out with "Mama" or "Dada," you got quite a response. Our language development and mental abilities are tied directly to memory, and so it may be helpful to explain briefly how your memory works.

If you think back to your first memories, they are probably very vivid, perhaps even traumatic. You might recall a particularly intense smell or sound, or certain colors.

Your first memory is probably of an experience that took place when you were three or four years old, because before that time your brain did not have a system into which information could be integrated. However, once you learned the relationship between cause and effect, how to talk and how to identify information and categorize it, your brain began to store memories rapidly.

This storage process, which takes place over the course of a lifetime, amounts to the sum and substance of who you are as a unique individual.

THE LIBRARY OF YOUR MIND

Someone once said, "The brain is a very big place in a very small space." Your brain is an unimposing gray mass that weighs approximately three pounds. Physically, it is hardly impressive. Yet this lumpy mass is the focal point of all human potential. For most people, it is almost impossible to fathom the storage capacity of the brain—which theoretically can hold *a hundred trillion* bits of information or hundreds of times more than the most sophisticated computers.

Your brain is constantly bombarded with information and, as it comes in, your brain filters, evaluates, associates, discards, and reevaluates that information in a sorting system that is unimaginably complex. Your memory is like a vast and brilliantly organized library of your experiences: everything meaningful that you have seen, smelled, tasted, touched, heard, and read. It is a mass of cells which contains the emotional responses you have had to different experiences in your life. It carries your hopes, fears, dreams, and aspirations.

As a behavioral psychologist, I try to investigate and understand people in terms of how well they function within their environment. Our memories have a direct bearing on this, because we remember the experiences and people and places and things that are meaningful, in a certain sense, to our survival. Indeed, it is our ability to adapt to our continually changing environment that assures our continued physical and emotional well-being.

It is easy to understand the adaptive aspect of memory and how it changes with age if we look at a newborn human or animal. Certainly the process is more dramatic in animals that are not protected and taught by their parents for extended periods. Many animals, for example, go from the security of the womb to an almost instant vulnerability. At a very young age they must face the dangers of the world alone, armed with only a few instinctive reflexes. The animal will face a barrage of new stimuli: colors, sounds, smells, and sensations. It must quickly develop a nose for what is important—how food can be found and how to avoid its enemies.

At first the young animal remembers everything—it does not know yet how to sort out what is meaningful and what is not. Very soon, though, it learns that a particular pattern of movement or sound can signal the presence of danger or the presence of food. It is adaptive, early in life, for the animal to remember an incredible amount of specific information. As it learns to detect patterns, however, the animal discerns what kind of information is important and what is irrelevant.

As human beings, we are continually looking for these patterns. We find patterns by comparing one situation to another and looking for the commonalities.

In memory training, we establish commonalities where they are often not naturally found.

DO WE REMEMBER EVERYTHING?

People often ask me if our brain stores everything that passes through it: every experience, every image, every smell, every person we meet. Even if it is an "info-byte" which we can never recall, is it still stored somewhere? My somewhat facetious answer is "What would be the point?"

Again, we look to the young animal, which begins to sort out what is important and what is not at an early age. If we had no filtering system, our minds would be under the constant assault of input—and we would be deluged with mostly meaningless information.

There is a fascinating case of a man named Shereshevskii (S), who seemed to remember everything. He used a process called synesthesia, which means he absorbed information through several different sensory systems at once, and with enormous accuracy. For S, information did not have to be meaningful to be remembered. He could remember poetry in foreign languages, scientific formulas with no intrinsic meaning to him— virtually anything one might present. But not only did he remember the primary information before him, but every sound, tone, and smell that was also present at the time. Therefore, if someone coughed while reading him a story, he would remember the cough. Interestingly, he could not remember names and faces—because the intricacies of facial features and changing expressions made it impossible to remember a face from one point to the next. Whether daily life was helped or hindered by this advanced process is debatable. But one can imagine a scenario where you simply could remember too much.

Most of us do not wrestle with too much memory. In normal human development, a certain amount of *selectivity* begins to set in when we are very young. For example, once we know that milk comes from a bottle, we don't have to remember the details of every feeding.

As we grow older, this kind of selective focusing becomes more so-phisticated. We focus on what we want or need to remember, whether it is learning the alphabet or that a hot flame can burn, or recalling a first date or a beautiful sunset.

Interestingly, in those patients I see who are severely depressed, the selectivity process has gone awry. These individuals are caught up in an involuntary process of focusing only on unpleasant or negative experi-ences—and their mood, as a result, is depressed.

For instance, a young man might have had basically caring, affectionate parents but can only recall the one or two times his parents might have criticized him harshly or restricted him overzealously. I've had patients tell me they are academic failures, and it is not unusual for the people who are telling me this to be renowned scholars or brilliant scientists. When you ask for evidence, they sometimes have to go back to third or fourth grade when they failed a particular test or did not know the answer to a specific question. While normal memory is adaptive to life, this selective negative memory certainly is not and in extreme depression can even lead to suicide.

It is important to emphasize that what is adaptive is not always what is most comfortable. There are painful lessons to be learned, and the mature individual bears this in mind.

The real answer to the question "Do we remember everything?" then, is no. We do not remember our lives unedited. For the most part—if we are healthy individuals—we remember what is adaptive to remember, whether it is a spouse's birthday or a dream. We store the information that is meaningful to us and cast off the rest.

Throughout this book we will examine the importance of meaningful information—because it is by making a memory or a person's name or the location of our glasses *meaningful* that we ensure proper storage. Sometimes this will involve "faking" it—dramatizing information to make it more enticing to our memory systems. But meaningfulness plays a major role in our memory training, and you will see its importance in the following chapters.

ALL MEMORIES ARE NOT CREATED EQUAL

We could see with the example of S that all individuals have different memory strengths and weaknesses. In a sense memory is like intelligence; there are people who are smart in different ways. You probably have heard about people with photographic memories, who are able to record complete images mentally and recall them with utter precision. These people are extremely rare.

On one occasion when my assessment team was in Italy demonstrating memory testing on a television show, we encountered a young man who seemed to possess this ability. There were about two hundred people in the audience, and he began asking for first names, seat after seat, row after row. He asked about a hundred people their names and was able to recall them without a mistake.

We were fascinated with his performance and asked if he wanted to take a basic assessment test live on national television. The test we gave him measures name and face association ability—the same test we are going to ask you to take later on.

Using a video, we presented a series of persons who introduced themselves and then we scrambled the order of the persons—and presented them again, without names. He was to furnish the names. His eyes narrowed, and suddenly it was apparent that he was in deep and troubled concentration. To his growing embarrassment, he began to err in his identifications. As it turned out, he not only failed to get a perfect score, but fell squarely into the average range.

As I instantly realized, the young man had a unique ability to remember names as they related to *spaces* the people occupied: he was memorizing the names and placing them in a kind of spatial order. But when asked to connect names to faces, he was no better than average. Most of us do not have our memory strengths and weaknesses revealed before millions of television viewers—and it's not something I would recommend. But it is important to know that each individual has an extraordinary array of memory strengths and weaknesses.

Interestingly, there is research that suggests that there are gender differences in memory. Women seem to have a greater ability to make name-face associations than men (though not on tasks involving only facial recognition), while men appear to have a marginally better facility to recall routes while traveling. Women also perform better on recalling lists and details of personal experiences. Some of these differences doubtlessly reflect cultural biases; your own experience might bear this out. In addition, you are probably aware if you have a special gift for remembering phone numbers or complicated directions or historical minutiae, like the names of all of the kings and queens of England.

Just as we have certain strengths, we also have certain weaknesses. If you're like most people, your weaknesses fall into the realm of the commonplace rather than the exotic. If you're one of those people who knows what it's like to have a mental blank or lose your keys or forget the name of the person you were just introduced to, you know precisely what I mean.

THE ROLE OF DESIRE

Having said this, I want to stress that a lot of memory weaknesses keel over in the face of desire. Memory strengths are related to intelligence— but not necessarily confined to it. On the Wechsler Adult Intelligence Scale, a standard intelligence test, four of the eleven tests given are directly related to memory, and the others rely on memory to one degree or another. Yet I have known people who score in the average or even below-average range on tests of intelligence but can rattle off the box scores and highlights of the last forty Baltimore Orioles' baseball games with complete accuracy. In almost every case, memory weaknesses can be overcome by sheer desire and interest.

With the proper motivation and some training, your memory can be improved in every single category—and without enormous effort.

SHORT- AND LONG-TERM MEMORY

At some point, you have no doubt heard about short- and long-term memory. The terms are used differently by different people, but there are at least two types of memory related to time, and understanding how each works could be helpful. Basically, the short- and long-term memories compose a librarylike system for taking in, storing, and retrieving information—and it is this system we will activate in the chapters ahead.

A great deal of information enters short-term memory, where it has a life expectancy calculated in seconds or minutes. When we talk about something going in one ear and out the other, this is where that swift migration takes place. The short-term memory is a terribly unreliable holding place because the slightest bit of interference can push the newly acquired information out of our consciousness. Say, for example, you have dialed 411 and gotten a phone number from the information operator—and suddenly the doorbell rings. Chances are your memory will be erased and that phone number will be lost.

Short-term memory also has a limited capacity: you can only hold a sequence of about seven unrelated bits of information at a time. This is an obvious convenience for remembering the traditional seven-digit phone number, for example. But seven pieces of information are not necessarily limited to seven digits.

Through a process called *chunking* you can remember many more numbers by grouping them into seven discrete groups of information. Take your Social Security number, for instance. Though it is a nine-digit number, you probably—without really thinking about it—chunk it into three groups when you are asked to recall it. Again, in short-term memory you can store about *seven* chunks at a time.

In trying to improve and empower our memories, the trick is to get the information we want planted into our short-term memory and then transferred to a meaningful place in our long-term memory.

Long-term memory is composed of different kinds of relatively permanent memories. These memories fall into three broad categories: *procedural memory* (like how to ride a bike), *knowledge memory* (like what a word means or mathematical verities such as $2 + 2 = 4$), and *specific factual memory*.

These three memory systems are, in a certain sense, independent of one another; one can be impaired while another is not. For instance, knowledge memory generally remains intact and continues to expand during the later decades of life, while memories for specific, unrelated facts may decline substantially.

Procedural memory is generally most resistant to forgetting. In a well-documented case, a psychologist once took a severely impaired patient with Alzheimer's disease out for a day of golf. The man was in his late seventies and had been an avid golfer throughout his adult life.

Although the man had no idea where he was, what year it was, or whether the President was Franklin Roosevelt or George Bush, he remembered the procedures used in playing golf. He selected the correct clubs and swung like an aging pro, although he had no idea of his score on each hole—or even that he had played previous holes. It was a graphic illustration of the independence of these three memory systems.

All of the material in your long-term memory is organized and cross-indexed, somewhat like a library. The indexing system works in this way: if you were playing intramural basketball when you learned over the public address system that President Kennedy was shot, your memory might be filed under President Kennedy, high school gymnasium, basketball, sadness/shock/fear, best friend crying—and the hundred and one other details of that episode.

The capacity of your long-term memory is virtually unlimited. You have tens of millions of memories stored in your long-term memory and most may never be destroyed or lost, though sometimes they seem impossible to retrieve.

In general, the more meaningful and dramatic an event is—the Kennedy assassination is a common example—the more likely it is to be stored and easily retrieved. This fact has broad implications for memory training. That is, by placing a relative value on a piece of new information, we either let it advance to long-term memory or allow it to recede from consciousness.

The challenge, for most of us, is to take the commonplace—like "where I just put my keys" or "what that man's name is"—and somehow make it vital and meaningful. In the course of a lifetime, one sets his keys perhaps thousands of different places and meets hundreds of new people. Much of this information never enters long-term memory because no association is formed or meaning attached to it. Often, if the information is to be recalled, artificial techniques must be employed.

For instance, suppose you generally place your keys next to a plant on the kitchen counter. By imagining that the plant is a Venus "key" trap

—and by animating the image in your mind—you suddenly have transformed a very mundane gesture, like tossing the keys onto the counter, into something more vivid, and therefore more meaningful. You also have created a new heading in your filing system that will stand out from the thousands of other key placements in your life.

When it comes to the memory issues that frustrate us the most, the problem we face is mostly one of filing and retrieval. As we become older, we often restrict what is filed to useful, global types of information. We may ignore an individual's name but store a great many useful facts related to his character and abilities. Unlike the Alzheimer's patient, however, healthy older adults have the capacity to remember as much specific information as twenty-year-olds—if they fool the generally adaptive information filtering system into filing this information as if it were critically important.

In future chapters, you will see how we can actually work within the confines of your short- and long-term memory systems to make memories more meaningful, vivid, and dramatic, so that you will almost effortlessly file them in more accessible places and thus improve your recall dramatically.

First, though, let's look at the flip side of how your memory works—and see just how forgetfulness takes place.

2

Why We Forget

A few years ago, I received a phone call from the wife of a fifty-six-year-old retired navy captain who recently had entered civilian life and was exhibiting some unusual behavior. Just a few days before, his boss had questioned him about a project in Ohio and the retired captain —a man whose reputation for competence was well known—had no idea what his boss was talking about.

He bluffed his way through the conversation, returned to his office, and went through his files. It didn't take long to find the bulging "Ohio" folders; they were filled with dozens of documents. As it turned out, he not only had spearheaded the project but had just returned from Ohio three weeks before. And he had been there for several days.

The man related this story to his wife and she became alarmed. She had noticed odd bouts of forgetfulness at home and was becoming concerned that a serious problem was developing. One evening, for example, she and her husband had gone out to dinner with another couple. After a convivial meal with old friends, her husband volunteered to retrieve the car and take everyone home. Instead, he drove off—stranding the people he had dined with only moments before.

Over the following months, I watched Alzheimer's disease dismantle the life of this vital man, a good husband and the father of four children. Six months after my first consultation with him, in which he angrily and often convincingly denied any problem—"I've never been good at names"; "I just wasn't trying"; "I never did well on tests"—he had become a weak and uncertain individual, wholly dependent on his wife, whose arm he gripped tightly wherever they went. Soon thereafter, he could not recognize his or her children. The complex set of memories that had made this man an individual had been destroyed.

As we grow older, many of us joke about getting Alzheimer's disease, but the jokes are usually accompanied by nervous laughter. Alzheimer's is a progressive, irreversible neurological disorder, and its primary symptom is memory loss. It has nothing to do with garden-variety forgetfulness, but the disease is so devastating that it nearly has become a national obsession.

The reasons for this have to do with America's changing demography. As recently as a hundred years ago, the life expectancy in this country was forty-six years for men and forty-eight years for women. Today, the average years are seventy-one and seventy-eight, respectively, and for the aging population, Alzheimer's is an authentic threat. Chances of getting the disease are as high as 20 percent for individuals who are eighty-five years or older. But it is important to note that for people like the retired captain, who are in their fifties and sixties, the chances of developing Alzheimer's are substantially less than one in one hundred.

SO WHY CAN'T I REMEMBER PEOPLE'S NAMES?

If you were born before the Korean War, chances are that in some respects, your memory is simply not what it used to be. It's a fact: in all mammalian species—including man—the ability to remember certain kinds of information declines with age. Most of what you are experiencing if you fall into the forty-years-plus category may simply be age-related memory impairment.

Some types of memory skills peak in the first or second decade of adult life, particularly those involving the ability to absorb information quickly and to do so in the midst of myriad distractions. These and other memory abilities may decline by 50 percent or more over an adult's life span.

Fortunately, this is not as discouraging as it sounds because other factors compensate. While you may not be able to keep as many balls in the air as you once could, the combination of wisdom, judgment, and knowledge more than make up for the decline in your speed of recall. Even more reassuring, sheer desire and the application of memory training techniques can make a dramatic difference in your ability to remember.

Indeed, people who seem as sharp as ever when they grow older are usually those who have consciously made an effort to overcome the effects of aging on memory.

COULD YOU SLOW DOWN A LITTLE?

The most profound change in memory skills that comes with age is the ability to take in information that is delivered quickly. Thinking may actually slow down. The *quality* of our thinking does not change but the *speed* at which we receive, absorb, and react to information may slow measurably. As we grow older, we really need more time to receive and sort information.

Ten years ago, for instance, your ability to remember a hastily delivered toll-free number on a late-night television announcement was probably better than it is today. Today you might forget the number before reaching the telephone—or you may not even grasp the number at all. This is hardly the end of the world; all it means is that you have to compensate for this memory deficit. What might you do? The obvious strategy here is to write the number down.

Sometimes, though, this slowing process is more difficult to live with. Several years ago I became friends with an insurance executive who made his fortune and retired at the age of fifty to pursue his lifelong ambition to become an economist. This is a man with a tremendous intellect. Yet during his first semester back in school, the man was in a daze. He kept telling me, "I can't keep up with these kids, I just can't keep up."

If I had run some comparative I.Q. tests on his peers at the university, I am confident that my friend would have been among the most gifted students intellectually. But this alone could not compensate for the speed at which the students in his classes were operating. He had to take meticulous notes, read them over two or three times, and sometimes paraphrase the material once more to make sure it had sunk in. These strategies and techniques might have been somewhat burdensome, but he was able then to participate—and in fact excel—as he pursued his lifelong quest.

CHEWING GUM AND WALKING
AT THE SAME TIME

As we get older, our ability to function amid distractions also decreases. The ability to concentrate varies from person to person, so *your* baseline will not be the same as the next person's; however, it is likely that you will experience a decline.

This means that ten or twenty years ago you might have been able to read the daily paper and intermittently listen to the evening news on television, but today you might need to focus solely on one of those activities.

I remember walking past my daughter Carolyn's bedroom when she was studying for her final exams. As I walked past her door, I could hear a pounding, squealing rock group—and she had earphones on! This was not what I was paying thousands of dollars in tuition for, so I walked in.

"Carolyn," I said, "I know you have finals next week and it's late. Either start studying or go to bed—but stop wasting your time listening to that music."

"But Dad, I am studying," she said, looking up from what I could see was a pile of books. Carolyn had been doing integral calculus.

It's not that I would ever want to listen to rock music and study calculus simultaneously, but somehow I got a flash of my own mortality in that little episode. At this point in my life, I cannot imagine being able to focus on something as demanding as calculus in less than a soundproof, padded cell. Losing the ability to focus successfully on a number of things at once is simply another part of the aging process, as natural as our first steps and first words.

This is not to say age is the *only* culprit when it comes to forgetfulness or distractedness. Sometimes circumstances make it impossible to concentrate. I remember I once delivered a lecture at a large pharmaceutical company on the topic of drug development for treatment of memory loss in older adults, a topic I knew extremely well. I was so comfortable with the materials that I felt no need to develop, much less read, a prepared text.

For the first few minutes everything went smoothly. However, five minutes into the material I looked into the audience of about three hundred people and noticed that people were speaking to each other, then looking toward me and laughing. Initially I thought it must be my imagination, but as more and more people appeared to be laughing I began to consider possible reasons for it: I tried subtly to check my clothing, ran my hand over my hair and face. Meanwhile, my lecture was not going so well. I began to stumble through the material and on several occasions completely lost track of where I was in my delivery. My face was flushed and I was perspiring. I managed to end the talk prematurely with a quick summary statement and slid down from the stage to sit in front of the still laughing audience.

At that point I looked up to see the source of the humor. Behind the podium was a clock with the company logo touting "consistent scientific progress" over minutes, hours, days, and years. The hands of the clock were spinning wildly out of control in one direction and then the other. I felt an instant sense of relief, and learned an important lesson about the effect of specific environmental circumstances on mental performance.

I doubt a twenty-year-old would have fared any better than I did in this situation, and he or she—for lack of experience—probably would have fared worse.

But the fact remains that if we *are* older, we must deliberately take measures to compensate for changes that occur in the brain—regardless of circumstance. If we are meeting people for the first time, for instance, we must take measures like those I will outline in following chapters to brand their names into our memories. If we are cooking and the phone rings, we better stare at the pot—or take the spoon with us—so as not to forget the food. If we are driving to a new place, we might not want to listen to our "How to Speak Italian" tapes at the same time.

THE NEED FOR MORE CUES

As we get older, we generally need more cues to trigger a memory. Probably the most famous cue in Western literature was the madeleine that inspired Proust's monumental *Remembrance of Things Past*. An old fifties song might trigger a set of memories for you, or the smell of a certain cologne.

When you were younger, someone might have asked you if you could remember the name of the lady who lived next door to you when you were growing up—and bingo, just like that, you might have recalled her name. Now you would probably need to know more in order to recall her: that she always made vegetable soup, her kitchen table had a red-checked cloth, her husband drove a Ford Fairlane. An entire word picture might be required, along with some time to think about it, before the name would pop back into your memory.

This holds true not just for distant memories but for the retrieval of new information as well. If you are visiting your hometown, for example, recall alone might not be enough anymore to get you where you want to go. You might need to make a point of remembering certain landmarks along the way.

This decline in your ability to remember is hardly catastrophic, and I would emphasize again that it in no way reflects on the quality of your intellect. In fact, your collected experience and knowledge is now substantially more valuable than it was at the tender age of twenty. But there are measures you must now use to get at that treasury of information. These are easy to learn and to employ, as you will see.

SOME PHYSIOLOGICAL AND PSYCHOLOGICAL REASONS WE FORGET

Age causes a good deal of forgetfulness. But there are other significant physiological and psychological factors (some of which are reversible) which can inhibit one's ability to remember.

• DEPRESSION. An individual's mood has a lot to do with his ability to remember, and we will talk more about this later on. Serious depression is more than a mood swing, though, and it can cause a high degree of forgetfulness. People who are seriously depressed are unable to concentrate on anything for more than a very brief period of time. When such people do take in information, it is usually the kind that supports their pain or boredom with life. Their behavior is maladaptive; it conspires to keep them in emotional jeopardy rather than health. This is not a voluntary process. Unless some kind of therapy is sought, people can be mired in this state for quite a long time.

I have worked with many depressed patients—young and old—who believe that they suffered from memory impairment and actually came to me because of their forgetfulness. When we began to unravel their situation, we discovered that depression was responsible for the memory loss —and began to work on that. In each case, when the depression lifted, memory function was restored. If this is a possibility for you, I would advise finding a counselor or therapist who can help you break through the causes of your depression.

• DRUGS AND ALCOHOL. It is commonly known that most people, after a heavy drinking binge, can't remember what they said or who they were with or where they were. Alcohol is an inhibitory drug: the relaxed feeling one gets when one is intoxicated is due in part to the breakdown of normal reasoning and thought processes, including the processing of information. Of course, this condition is reversed when the person awakens the next morning and alcohol has been eliminated from his system. However, people who drink inordinate amounts of alcohol over a period of time can suffer from a type of amnesia known as Korsakoff's syndrome, which is not reversible.

Drugs, too, can bring about memory loss. In our first consultation with a patient, my team and I thoroughly review his drug medication program, because sometimes a particular drug or combination of drugs can create memory deficiencies.

Anxiolytics (anti-anxiety medications), certain sleeping pills, muscle relaxants, some arthritis medications, and cortisone treatments can affect memory and cognition.

Also, any drug with a depressant effect can create memory problems. For instance, some high-blood-pressure medications have depressive side effects. Even antihistamines (like Benadryl) with warnings about operating heavy machinery or an automobile can have a temporary effect on memory.

Sometimes all that is required is a change of dosage or a substitution of one drug for another to eliminate the effects of these drugs on memory. If you are taking any of the drugs just mentioned and are troubled by your memory problems, I advise you to consult your physician.

Finally, smoking causes all sorts of degenerative diseases, but it also increases the risk of chronic obstructive lung disease. This disease cuts off oxygen to the brain cells—and may cause a serious decrease in brain function. If you are suffering from this disease and are having difficulties with memory, check with your physician.

• VITAMIN DEFICIENCY. If you are lacking in B-complex vitamins, particularly vitamin B_{12}, you can suffer from a debilitating condition that includes loss of memory. You can overcome B_{12} deficiencies by supplementing your diet with eggs, fish, meats, milk, and, of course, supplemental vitamin tablets. Although vitamin deficiencies may cause memory loss, a severe lack of vitamins is quite rare in the United States. Contrary to many claims, there is no sound evidence indicating that high doses of vitamins can improve memory in persons without deficiencies. Indeed, high doses can pose serious risks. If you believe you are suffering from some kind of vitamin deficiency, I recommend you consult with your physician.

• OUTRAGEOUS EXPECTATIONS. Many times when we forget things, we have a hard time accepting that we are less than perfect. A good number of my patients fall into the category of being young and upwardly mobile, and this group in particular seems to have a hard time accepting its limitations and its inability to control everything. The response of people like this, generally, is to apply an inordinate amount of pressure on themselves, which only worsens their performance. The simple solution is, of course, to take it easy. And it works.

• Stress. Obviously, inflated expectations are closely related to stress. Later on you'll see how this is a major factor when it comes to forgetting names. But before we get into a full discussion of stress and one result—inattentiveness—it might be helpful to see where our specific name-remembering technique fits into the overall scheme of memory training.

3

Memory Strategies 101

People who are skeptical about memory training generally believe that it is new or gimmicky, some kind of parlor trick at best. Nothing could be further from the truth. Memory strategies have been around for centuries, not only because forgetfulness is as old as man, but because before the dawn of the printed word an even greater premium was placed on one's ability to memorize. Indeed, in Greek and Roman culture, memory training was considered as much a part of the core curriculum for the educated man as rhetoric and mathematics.

Most scholars credit the Greek poet Simonides with the introduction of the memory arts. As the story goes, Simonides was to present his poetry at a banquet hall filled with distinguished guests. Midway through the banquet he was called out of the room. Just as he left, the building collapsed. Not one of the guests survived.

After the rubble had been cleared, Simonides was asked by grieving relatives to identify the crushed bodies, which were no longer recognizable. Simonides was able to do so by recalling where each person had been seated at the banquet. Using the elements of order and placement,

Simonides made the important discovery that spatial cues could trigger memory. This discovery gave rise to the method of loci, which uses location as a means of fixing a person, place, or thing in memory. It was the first memory training technique reported in Western history.

Simonides' method of loci was especially useful to Greek and Roman orators, who would associate different portions of their speech with different rooms in a house or building, yielding phrases like "in the first place" and "in the second place." Using this simple strategy, the historian Cicero was able to recite his speeches in the Roman Senate for several days without consulting notes.

Throughout Western history the most respected scholars and intellectuals—from Aristotle to Saint Thomas Aquinas—practiced the memory arts. Once the printed word became more accessible, memory arts were considered less important. However, with the ethic of the 1980s, where mental fitness became a tool for getting ahead, the quest for sharpened memory skills was revived. Today mental fitness is becoming as sought-after as physical fitness, and memory training courses are becoming a popular mainstream pursuit.

WHAT ARE MNEMONICS?

You probably have heard or read the word *mnemonics* before (the first *m* is silent). Basically, mnemonics are any method or technique that enhances your ability to remember. Most mnemonic devices are simple, even simplistic, since that is the whole idea behind easing recollection.

The specific mnemonic device that's been shown to work best for remembering people's names is called *association-exaggeration*, whereby connections are made between unlike things in order to make the commonplace more memorable and meaningful. We will, of course, go into detail about this later on. But first it might be useful to take inventory of the other basic memory weapons you may already have in your arsenal.

☞RHYMES

One of the easiest memory devices we all use is rhymes, and one of the most often used mnemonics begins, "Thirty days has September"—the short verse which is used to remember the months that have thirty days and those that have thirty-one. Other rhymes that you might remember are "*i* before *e*, except after *c*" or "Stalagmites stand up with all their might and stalactites hold on tight" or "One big *T* equals teaspoons three."

Word games associated with rhyming are memorable in phrases like "Stationary stands still, stationery is used for letters" or "Principal is a pal and a principle is a rule."

☞ACRONYMS

U.S.A. is the acronym for the United States of America. In memory training, an acronym uses the first letter of each word to be remembered and converts it into a word of its own. People who want to remember the names of the colors of the spectrum, for instance, use *ROY G. BIV* to remember "red, orange, yellow, green, blue, indigo, and violet."

College students use this technique in studying for tests, because so often they are required to memorize reams of information. An acronym can go a long way in holding information that is otherwise difficult to assemble into a meaningful mental arrangement.

Some other acronyms you might be familiar with are *HOMES* to remember the Great Lakes, or *SOS* for "Save Our Ship," or *SNAFU* for "Situation Normal, All Fouled Up."

☞ACROSTICS

This technique is a cousin to acronyms, and the best-known device is "Every Good Boy Does Fine" for the lines on the treble clef: E, G, B, D, F. In this case, you reverse the acronym process and take letters you need to remember and form a word or sentence.

Acrostics are also used for spelling, as in the spelling of *arithmetic* ("A Red Indian Thought He Might Eat Taffy In Church") or *geography* ("George Edward's Old Grandmother Rode A Pony Home Yesterday").

☞REPETITION

Repetition is necessary in the application of most mnemonics. But it is not sufficient on its own, except for in very short-term tasks, like repeating a telephone number several times after hearing it.

☞THE LINK-CHAIN SYSTEM

This technique is used to remember lists. One takes a list—for instance, pencils, oranges, flour, and dog biscuits—and visualizes each item to be remembered, then links each visually: pencils might be piercing oranges, then snowed upon by flour and snowballing into a pile of dog biscuits.

☞THE STORY SYSTEM

The story system uses the same concept as the link-chain system, but creates a story instead: "Once upon a time there were twelve marching *pencils* who encountered a beautiful field of *oranges.* Suddenly it began snowing *flour,* and all you could hear were barking *dog biscuits."* These kinds of systems employ the use of drama and exaggeration to make a common shopping list quite meaningful. As you will recall, one of the goals of memory training is to give shape and meaning to the commonplace.

☞FEINSTEIN FOOLPROOF METHOD

This method is used for telephone numbers only and employs the use of letters to make the digits more meaningful. Not long ago, telephone exchanges were the beneficiaries of this system; numbers would use words like *Niagara, Scarsdale, Weston* for the exchange, and the first two letters would correspond to the first two numbers (NI—64, SC—72, WE—93). Companies now use this method to make their toll-free numbers more meaningful, like 1-800-CARPETS. If you've ever seen a mnemonics performer wile his audience with his ability to remember an entire phone book, this is how he does it.

☞THE EIGHT-SECOND WINDOW

Studies have found that with eight seconds of pure, uninterrupted attention you can most reliably depend on a transfer from short- to long-term memory. So if you use the technique of simply paying attention—a valid technique for many people—you should do it for at least eight seconds, and possibly in concert with some of the other strategies just detailed.

You probably were surprised to note how many of the mnemonic devices just described you already use in daily life without thinking twice about it. Once you realize that these little tricks are not as strange as they might seem at first glance, you are ready to proceed to the technique of association-exaggeration, especially as it applies to remembering names and faces. We will tackle this technique in the following chapter.

4

Winning the Name Game I:

THE ART OF PAYING ATTENTION

Imagine this: You have been given an opportunity to present a bold idea to five people at the executive level of your company, and if they like it, chances are you're in for a promotion. You've only made three or four presentations in your career, but you know that your idea is solid and your immediate superior has been very encouraging. "Unless you walk in there with a Groucho Marx disguise on, you've got a done deal," he assures you.

You enter the conference room briskly. You are wearing a new suit, a power tie, and a fresh haircut. Introductions are made. You look each executive in the eye. You give a firm, decisive handshake to each one. You make your presentation and it flows like water. At the end, Sam Briggs, executive vice president of the company, congratulates you. "This was superb, Bates," he says. "Just hand all of your material over to Wallace, who will make the final decision. She'll be back to you on Thursday." Wallace? You look blankly at the three female faces in the room. Which one is Wallace?

IT'S NOT REALLY A
MEMORY PROBLEM AT ALL

When you are wrestling with a forgotten name ten seconds after an introduction is made, you are the victim of inattentiveness. You do not have a problem with a faulty memory, you have a problem with paying attention. *The fact is, you didn't see or hear the person in the first place.* And this is precisely what happened to the businessman who could not identify Ms. Wallace.

Inattentiveness and *stress* can create a powerful double-edged sword, and they generally are present in any social or business situation where you are meeting people for the first time.

Inattentiveness does not necessarily mean you are not paying attention; it means, most often, that you are paying attention to the wrong thing. You are focused on something *besides* the name and face that you want to learn. Add stress to that situation, and it is easy to see why you can walk away from a room full of people and not know a single name.

GETTING OUT OF YOURSELF
AND INTO THE PICTURE

Let's face it, the primary reason we fail to pay attention to a name is because we are paying attention to ourselves. Remember the last time you walked into a room of strangers? Probably the last thing on your mind was thinking that you had to make a conscious effort to remember people's names. Instead you were doubtlessly thinking about how you looked or what you were wearing. Or what about that firm handshake? The all-imperative eye contact?

The businessman in our example paid no attention to the very people whose approval he sought. His attention was solely on his own performance. As a result, he found himself in a very awkward situation that could have been completely avoided if only he had done some preparation.

As an illustration of how fragile the mind can be under such circumstances, I remember a trip I once took to Stockholm, where I was to address a conference of memory scholars on the neurochemistry of memory. I was with an associate, who happened to notice on the way to the conference center that I had on two mismatched socks. "Stop at a clothing store and get yourself a new pair," she advised. "Otherwise you'll be thinking about your socks throughout your entire speech." But I was tough and tossed off her idea as vanity.

The conference center was packed and, instead of what I thought would be about a hundred people in the audience, there were about six hundred. The man who introduced me made me out to be some kind of genius, and I was a little embarrassed. As I walked up to the podium under the glare of a huge spotlight, all I could think about was my socks.

Did it ruin my speech? Not totally. But I must say that the speech got off to a slow and rather awkward start, and I had to struggle to remember what I wanted to say—which was doubly embarrassing since I was addressing a conference of memory scholars. After my speech, my associate handed me a note, which simply read: "You should have bought the socks."

The point is that there are many simple things you can do to improve your ability to remember names that have nothing to do with memory techniques but everything to do with creating the most hospitable atmosphere for taking in information and retaining it. Following are a few guidelines that will help you concentrate and focus the next time you are presented with a new name and face to remember.

RULE #1:

MAXIMIZE YOUR COMFORT ZONE

The novelty of a new banquet hall or office or hostess's dining room adds a subtle stress to even the most enjoyable circumstances, and you must be ready for it. Your goal is to get all of the surface considerations well out of the way so you can concentrate on names and faces rather than your crooked tie or uneven hemline.

Therefore, rule number one is prepare for your situation.

• Make sure you feel comfortable and presentable in what you are wearing, so you can forget about it when you enter a new situation.

• Do your homework. If you are going to attend a business meeting or social event, call ahead for names and titles, if appropriate. If you are hearing a name for a second time, you are at a distinct advantage. To the best of your ability, be able to answer the question "Who's going to be there?" as thoroughly as possible before the occasion.

• Decide what you're *not* going to pay attention to. Don't think about your handshake or eye contact or what the room looks like. (In all probability the person you are meeting is suffering from inattentiveness and won't notice much about you, anyway.)

• Make a plan. Decide before an event who you are going to pay attention to and forget about the rest. If, for example, you say to yourself "I am going to be very conscious of the boss's wife's name," you'll do it.

Remember that most of the time introductions go so fast that if you're paying attention to anything else—even for a split second—you'll miss it.

RULE #2:

STAY IN THE PRESENT

When we fail to pay attention, it's usually because we are focusing on something else (usually ourselves) or are off in space somewhere. Let's talk a little bit about staying in the present moment.

Some of us are by nature easily distracted. This is a function of personality and is no reflection on intellect. We all have heard of the absent-minded professor, a genius in the abstract but hard-pressed to find his glasses in the morning. For people who are easily distracted, remembering names and faces can be a trial—because the slightest bit of interference throws them off.

Even if you are the kind of person who can function well in the midst of myriad distractions, a special kind of concentration is required when you are meeting people for the first time. It you try to focus on too much, you overload; if you don't focus on enough, you gain no information. The key is to strike a happy medium. Again, common sense is the strategy that is truly called for.

• When you meet a person, look at him or her. This may sound simplistic, but chances are you don't really look at the people you meet right now. Study their faces as you are listening to their name.

• If your mind wanders while you are meeting someone and you suddenly remember that you forgot to call the plumber back, stop everything. Start over. Saying "I'm sorry, I missed your name. Would you kindly repeat it?" will save you an evening of potential embarrassment.

• Consciously think about closing all of the doors to your mind and plunge yourself into the present moment. This takes practice but the results will give you a new sense of self-control and effectiveness.

When you are distracted, the associative pathways of your brain are simply taking you down a new course—sometimes this is a help, sometimes it is a hindrance. The problem is that too many tangents in a social situation can scatter your mental energy and render you lost. These tangents are part of life; in the course of writing this book, for example, I crumpled a piece of paper and tossed it into the wastebasket, silently awarding myself two points. Before I knew it, I was combing the sports section of the *Washington Post* for details of last night's Bullets game.

RULE #3:

YOU'VE GOT TO WANT IT

Motivation is crucial to any significant change in behavior. This goes for losing weight or quitting smoking or saving money—everything that requires some discipline and effort. I hope you don't place memory training in the same category as dieting, because what I am about to show you has a solid measure of fun and gamesmanship, while dieting is, well, dieting.

To show you the power of motivation, suppose I asked you to memorize ten grocery items: say, napkins, eggs, sugar, tea bags, coffee, apples, bread, butter, bacon, and milk. You probably would do a so-so job.

Now: **What if I offered you $1,000 to get a majority of the words on that list correct?** Do you think your performance would have been any stronger?

Motivation doesn't always come in the form of money, but it can make a profound difference in our ability to remember. If you have a low interest level in remembering someone's name, no amount of threats or arm twisting will cause you to pay attention.

On the other hand, if you have a serious interest in someone's name, that name will be almost impossible to forget. The bachelor at the company Christmas party who has longed to meet the attractive brunette from the seventh floor will most decidedly remember her name when they are introduced. The same goes for the salesperson who has been trying to land an important account with company X and discovers he has just met the president's wife.

But motivation does not always come so naturally. Sometimes one even has to "fake" interest and convince oneself that remembering a name is important, like it or not.

Obviously, your involvement in this book shows that you care about improving your memory skills—whether it is to improve your performance in business or to avert that annoying feeling of being in the middle of a conversation and "blanking out."

RULE#4:

THE ROSE-COLORED GLASSES FACTOR

Each of us is unique and it goes without saying that there are people, places, and things which would be more memorable to you than they would be to someone else. Two different people meeting someone new for the first time, for instance, may come away with totally different opinions about that person. Both might be right; they were just focusing on different things. It is not difficult to see that what is old to one person might seem distinguished to another; or that what seems deceitful to you might seem tactful to someone else.

This applies directly to what registers and what doesn't when you are meeting someone for the first time, and it's helpful to get a sense of your own particular vantage point. For instance, professional experience can affect your perspective positively and negatively. The maître d' of a fine restaurant will have a leg up on the biochemist with name-face association, simply because his profession calls for him to see and identify people all day long. An investment banker may be able to run through a spread sheet and rattle off his findings with complete accuracy a month later, while a novelist might see the same set of numbers as only a mass of unmemorable digits.

In any business or social situation, it is crucial to understand that your own predispositions may or may not serve you well when it comes to getting a name. The tools in the chapters ahead will help you to pay attention and work *with* your perspective rather than against it.

5

Winning the Name Game II:

THE TECHNIQUE

As I mentioned in the previous chapter, the association-exaggeration technique for remembering people's names has in our experience proved the most effective for the greatest number of people.

The pages you are about to read and the test you are about to take represent the core of the entire book. To get started, try to create an atmosphere in which you can focus undisturbed. If you are likely to be interrupted, wait until another time. Do whatever is required to establish the environment that you need to concentrate.

We will begin with a quick exercise. *You will need a clock or watch with a second hand, and a pencil.*

FIRST EXERCISE

On the facing page, you see nine faces and first names. I would like you to give yourself one minute to review the names and faces, and I suggest that as you look at each face, you repeat the name associated with it out loud. Try to absorb each of the names and faces. If you are ready, please begin.

REVIEW THE NAMES AND FACES

Thomas

Bruce

Patricia

Charles

Ruth

Susan

Diane

Leonard

Michael

IDENTIFY AS MANY AS YOU CAN

Now please fill in as many names as you can remember.

Let's see how you did. Go back and check the names against the faces and tabulate the number of answers that were correct. If you like, you can measure your performance against others in the same age category by consulting the scale on the next page.

CHECK YOUR PERFORMANCE

Your ability to remember names and faces is affected by age. The scale that follows will give you a sense of how well you did on the test you just took. Later on, you will be able to test your skills again, using the technique you are about to learn.

FIRST EXERCISE

If your age is between	the normal range of correct responses is:
18 and 39	4–8
40 and 49	3–7
50 and 59	3–6
60 and 69	2–5
70 and 89	1–4

THE TECHNIQUE

In the previous chapters, we discussed the importance of paying attention and minimizing distractions. But life *is* distracting, and when you enter a novel situation like a cocktail reception or a sales conference or even a PTA meeting, you are even more vulnerable to distractions.

Frankly, the exercise you just participated in was unrealistic. When was the last time you met a Thomas or Charles or Diane or Patricia who didn't say a word back to you? Or who didn't mind you staring intently at them for a minute or two?

And even though you were simply staring at a page in a book, weren't you a bit intimidated and concerned about your performance? If there is stress involved in looking at some faces and names on a page in the privacy of your own home, think how much pressure you are under when you are functioning in the outside world.

Meeting new people is stressful, no matter who you are or how many times you've done it. To counteract the stress of the situation, we must go to what might seem extraordinary lengths to lock a name and face into our memories. The five-step plan that follows is designed for individuals in real-life situations, and you can start using it immediately.

STEP ONE:

PICK AN OUTSTANDING FEATURE

The first step to remembering a name and face is to *get the face.*

To practice, look at a photograph of your spouse or a parent, or even a face from a magazine. Study it. Is there something particularly strange or interesting or attractive (or even ugly) about the face? Is the hair bright red and wavy? Are the eyebrows heavy? Are the eyes small and beady? Select one, and only one, outstanding feature—and stick with it.

Now commit that feature to memory by exaggerating it or animating it. If it is red and wavy hair, set it on fire in your mind's eye. If the eyebrows are bushy, see them wriggling. If the eyes are small and beady, have them dart this way and that.

If *nothing* jumps out at you, arbitrarily choose a feature. Here are some possibilities:

- Hair (volume, color, texture, hairline, length)
- Nose (size, width, sloped, bumpy, hawkish)
- Mouth (size, shape, lip size, teeth, smile)
- Cheeks (rounded [like a chipmunk's], defined cheekbones)
- Eyes (size, spacing, color, position, shape)

If you are having some difficulty focusing, think how you would describe this person as a witness or for a police artist's rendition. If there is nothing unique about the person's face, don't be concerned. You can transform this person's plain appearance or drabness into a strong visual impression.

Locking into the person's face is the most challenging part of the name-face association process. But it is vital that you not only pick an outstanding feature but animate or exaggerate this feature—to embed it in your memory. Remember, you have met hundreds of people in your lifetime and it is crucial that you instruct your brain that *this face is different, this face is important, this face must be remembered.* And the most effective way to communicate that is to give the face drama, even if it is artificial.

The first few times you do this, you might feel uncomfortable or silly —and it might even be difficult to pick an outstanding feature in the beginning. More than anything, practice will rid you of this self-consciousness.

STEP TWO:

GET THE NAME

You now have committed to memory an outstanding feature. Your next step is to get the name. You had an instant or two to get the feature, but largely you did it at your own pace. Getting the name is another story, because you are dependent on whomever is introducing you, and that person's timetable.

Follow these basics:

• Block out all other conversations around you, or thoughts about your own appearance or what you will say next.

• If you do not hear the person's name correctly, *immediately* ask him or her to repeat it.

• Repeat the name, either to yourself or, better yet, out loud: "It's a pleasure to meet you, Jack."

• Keep in mind that the factor most responsible for forgetting a name is failing to store the name in the first place.

• Whenever possible, control the timing and length of new introductions. For example, if you are conducting a meeting, you could ask each person to provide additional information about himself, thereby allowing yourself time to apply the technique.

STEP THREE:

TRANSFORM THE NAME TO A CONCRETE IMAGE

You've picked an outstanding feature and you've captured the name. You were able to animate or exaggerate the facial feature to make it more memorable. But what do you do with a name like Jack? How can you make the name Jack memorable?

Commonplace names are generally a problem, and most names *are* commonplace. When we refer to generic Americans, we call them John or Jane Doe. But that appellation could just as easily be Fred and Margaret Smith. Or Harry and Betty White. Unless you are meeting a Horatio or Desdemona for the first time, chances are you're going to forget that name immediately.

This is where, again, we infuse drama into the ordinary. By giving a name a dramatic association, you make it more memorable. This can be done by rudimentary and even amusing connections.

For example, if you met the generic Fred Smith we've just mentioned and you suddenly envisioned Fred Astaire in a blacksmith's outfit, you'd have to work hard to get Fred Smith out of your mind.

Put Princess Margaret or Margaret O'Brien in that same blacksmith's outfit, standing next to Fred, and try to forget those names. *You can't.*

Try a few more. Harry and Betty White. You could imagine Harry Truman, in your mind's eye, dressed in white. How about Betty Crocker, also dressed in white? Using whatever association comes easiest and most quickly to you, you can implant the person's name in your memory.

Whenever possible, use an easy recognition method. Here are some examples:

- Color (Jeffrey Black)
- Occupation (Nicholas Carpenter)
- City or place (Matthew Houston)
- Name brand or company (Joan Reynolds)
- Well-known personality or event
  —sports (Billie Jean Matthews)
  —politics (Gregory Carter)
  —actor, actress (Susan Olivier)
  —historical (William Washington)
- Animals (Gloria Katz)
- People you already know

Or you can use the substitute word method:

- Use phonics, a word that sounds like the name you want to remember (Joan, phone; Robert, robber).

Chapter 6 is devoted to the most commonly used first and last names, and provides excellent words on which to peg them. If you turn quickly to page 61, you can scan the names and cues to get a sense of the easy-to-learn possibilities. One caveat: a small percentage of people memorize the cues so well that they forget the names associated with them. I remember, for instance, a trainee who walked up to a woman named Catherine and called her "Cat"! Once you are aware of this pitfall, you can avoid it by emphasizing the name mentally, rather than the cue.

STEP FOUR:

LINK THE IMAGE OF THE NAME TO THE DISTINCTIVE FEATURE

Now you have a feature and a name, both of which you have given dramatic associations. The crucial fourth step is to make a conscious, clear visual association between the feature and the name.

To do this, place the image of the name upon the distinct feature and allow your creative side to take over. Keep the following in mind:

• If you make the image active you will increase recall. For instance, upon meeting Dennis, who has a long face, substitute a tennis racquet for his long face. A woman named April who has beautiful blue eyes might be recalled this way: increase the size of her eyes and turn them into blue clouds of rain (April showers!). Or for a man named Dave who has short wavy brown hair, picture his brown hair turning to blue waves moving across his head.

• Don't be put off by bizarre images that come to your mind; actually, the stranger the better. On the other hand, it is not *necessary* to come up with strange ideas. If you feel uncomfortable with a bizarre image—and this might be true for you in an important business situation—use a natural, interactive image.

STEP FIVE:

REVIEW

At first glance, it might seem like this encoding process takes hours instead of a few minutes. Unquestionably, your first attempts will be clumsy and time-consuming, but you will see after just a few tries that you will pick up speed and versatility. Your imagination might seem stiff and unyielding now, but once you let go, you will find dozens of images at your disposal.

But the final key to remembering a person's name permanently is *review*. This doesn't have to be formal; it actually works best if you repeat the name out loud at the end of your conversation—"I am so glad we finally had a chance to meet, Jack"—while concentrating on the distinctive feature and image. This is particularly important when a substitute word like *phone* for Joan or *robber* for Robert is used. It enables you to store the proper name, preventing situations in which you recall the substitute instead of the name!

Finally, there is no reason not to write down a person's name. If it is important for your business, you can write down the name and perhaps a few notes about appearance and facts about family, hobbies, business perspective, or career history. Many people use business cards or Rolodex files for this purpose.

Example: Jack Hellman, white wavy hair, jacks, Hellmann's mayonnaise; wife's name is Eleanor; children are Jack, Jr., and Lilly; profession: real estate; knows Fred Barnes; sailor

PUTTING IT ALL TOGETHER

The best way to practice the five-step plan for remembering people's names is to start with people on televised news or in magazines, as well as the people you meet. At your own pace, you can adapt the principles of the method to your own taste and strengths. For instance, I know some people who can get away with just remembering names; they don't have to concentrate too much on faces because their visual powers are so strong. For other people, whose verbal powers dominate, the key is to study faces and invent wild animations; the names are simply no problem.

If you like, you can do the following exercise and try to put into practice the five-step plan—or your own version of it.

Remember: get the face, read the name, get an association for the name, combine the two—and review.

Compare your performance to the first exercise in this chapter. Chances are you will improve on your very first attempt.

Again, *you will need a pencil, and a watch or clock with a second hand.*

FOLLOW-UP EXERCISE

Please study the faces and names on the following pages. Use the technique, to the best of your ability, and do not forget to say each name out loud. You have one minute to study the faces.

FIRST TRY

Timothy

Marilyn

John

Barbara

Helen

Roger

Larry

Sally

Alice

IDENTIFY AS MANY AS YOU CAN

Now please fill in the names of every person you can remember. *When you are finished, please go to the next page without calculating your score.*

SECOND TRY

Look at the names and faces again. Study them, using the technique, for one minute. Then turn the page and fill in as many names as possible.

Larry

Alice

Timothy

Roger

John

Helen

Barbara

Marilyn

Sally

CHECK YOUR PERFORMANCE

Please calculate the number of correct answers on the Follow-up Exercise and see how well you performed by looking at the scale that follows.

FIRST TRY

If your age is between	the normal range of correct responses is:
18 and 39	4–8
40 and 49	3–7
50 and 59	3–6
60 and 69	2–5
70 and 89	1–4

SECOND TRY

If your age is between	the normal range of correct responses is:
18 and 39	6–9
40 and 49	5–9
50 and 59	4–9
60 and 69	3–7
70 and 89	1–6

IDENTIFY AS MANY AS YOU CAN

Please fill in as many names as possible.

Go back and check the names against the faces and tabulate the number of correct answers. You can measure your performance against others using the scale on page 59.

6

The Most Common American Names

I f you take only one thing from this book, make it the contents of this chapter.

On the following pages, you will find 60 male and female names, composing more than 50 percent of the American names in common usage. With each name, you will find a cue to help you visualize the name. The cue may be a synonym or a sound-alike or simply a vivid rhyming word.

The more names and cues you remember, the more effective you will be at your next meeting, reception, or party. *It is that simple.*

My advice is to memorize a few names at a time. Use famous people or people you know well to make the connections and to practice. As you will see, there are photographs provided to help you visualize the cue on an actual face. Don't skip over this vital step. It will enhance your ability to remember names and faces significantly. Here, then, are the names and faces . . . and cues.

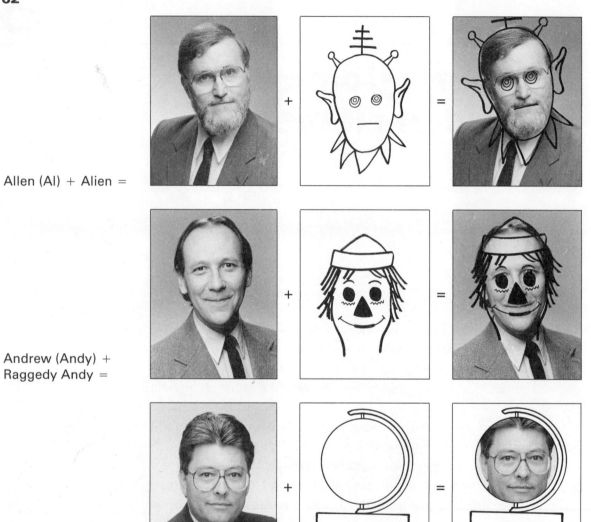

Allen (Al) + Alien =

Andrew (Andy) +
Raggedy Andy =

Anthony (Tony) +
Tony Award =

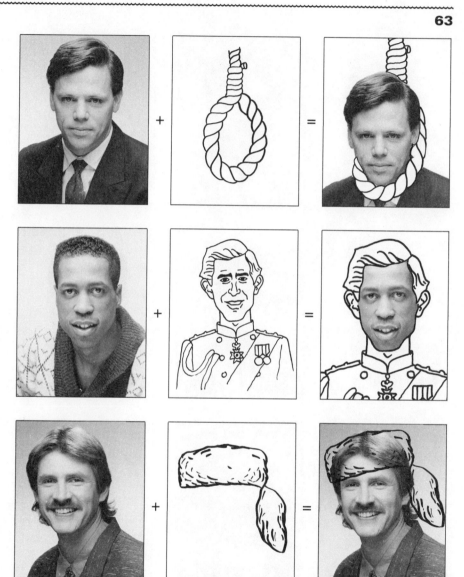

Bruce + Noose =

Charles (Chuck) +
Prince Charles =

Daniel (Dan) +
Daniel Boone =

David (Dave) +
Shave =

Donald (Don) +
Don Juan =

Douglas (Doug) +
Douglas MacArthur =

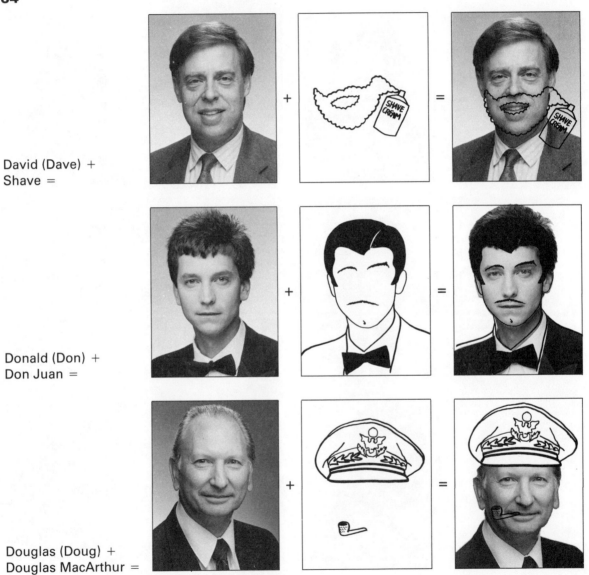

Edward (Ed) +
Bed =

Francis (Frank) +
Frankenfurter =

Frederick (Fred) +
Dead =

George + George
Washington =

Henry (Hank) +
Henry the Eighth =

Howard (Howie) +
"How!" =

Jack + Ball &
Jacks =

James (Jim) +
Chains =

John + Long
Johns =

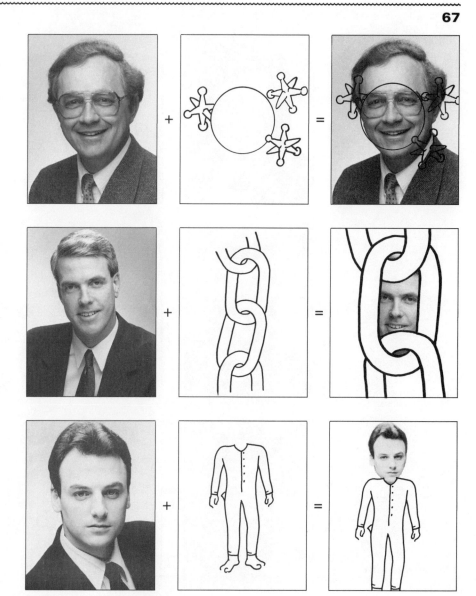

Joseph (Joe) +
Toe =

Mark +
Checkmark =

Matthew (Matt) +
Doormat =

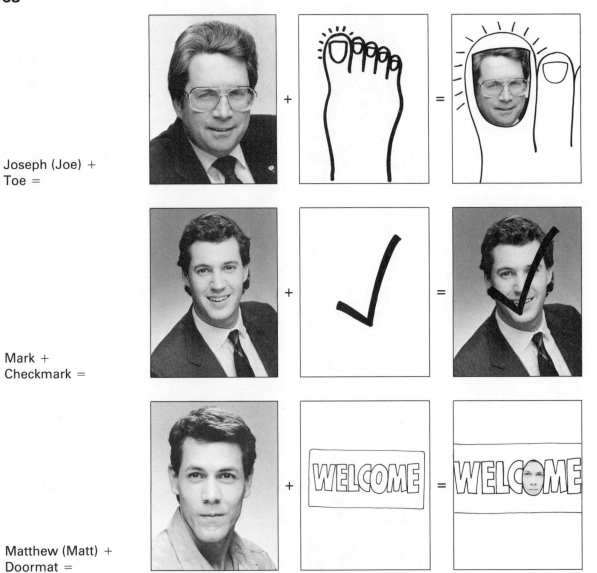

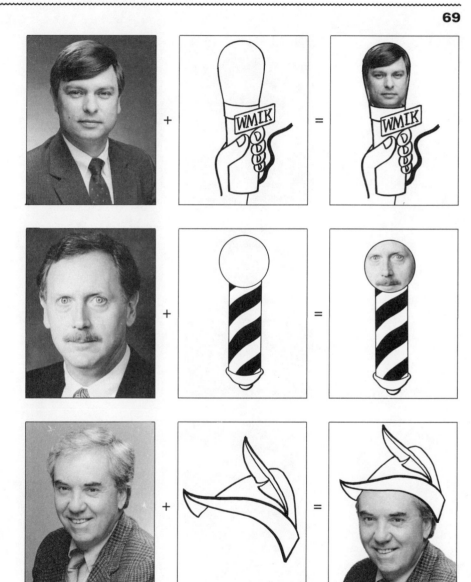

Michael (Mike) +
Mic(rophone) =

Paul + Pole =

Peter (Pete) +
Peter Pan =

Phillip (Phil) +
Pill =

Richard (Rick) +
Richard Nixon =

Robert (Rob) +
Robber =

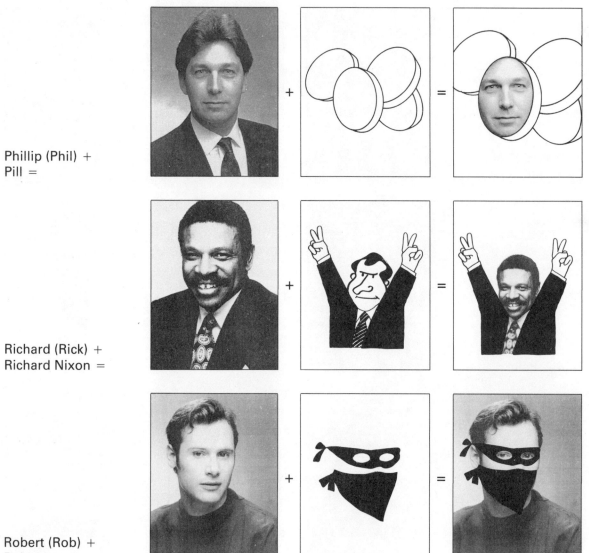

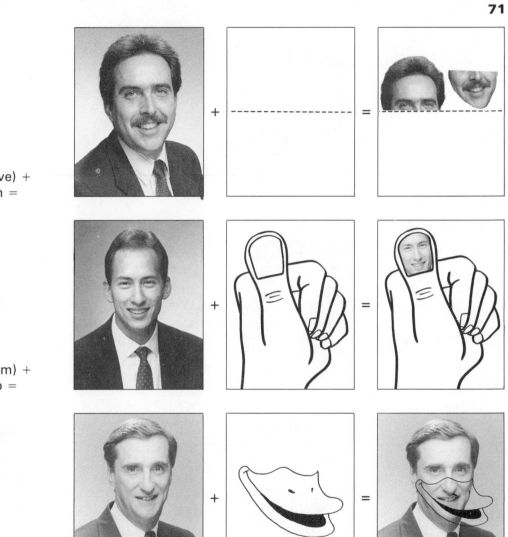

Steven (Steve) +
Even Steven =

Thomas (Tom) +
Tom Thumb =

William (Bill) +
Duck's Bill =

Alice + Alice in
Wonderland =

Amy + Aim =

Anne +
Raggedy Ann =

Barbara +
Barbie Doll =

Carolyn
(Carol) + Caroler =

Catherine
(Katy) + Cat =

Christine (Chris) +
Christmas Tree =

Deborah (Debbie,
Deb) + Debutante =

Diane +
Princess Di =

Donna +
Madonna =

Elizabeth +
Queen Elizabeth =

Gail + Gale =

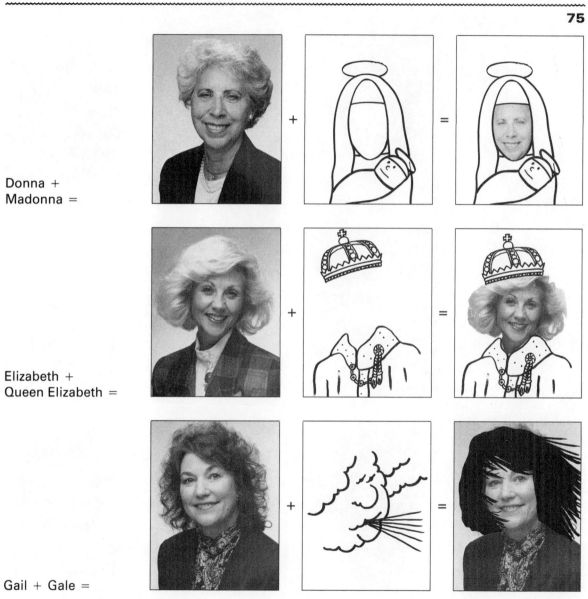

Helen + Hell =

Jane + Chain =

Jeanne (Jean) +
Blue Jeans =

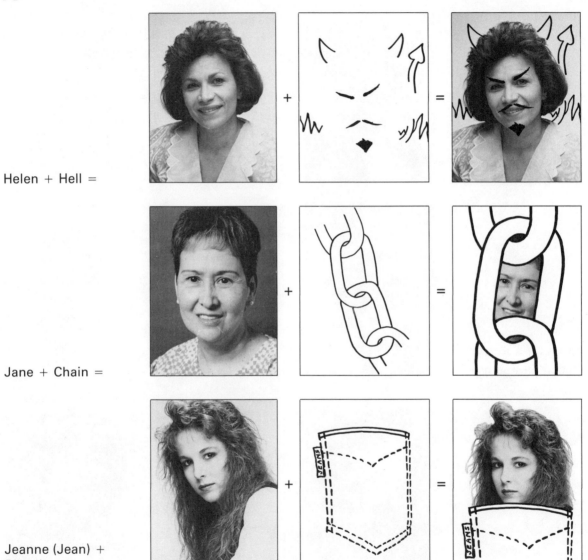

Jennifer (Jenny) +
Penny =

Joan + Phone =

Karen + Carrot =

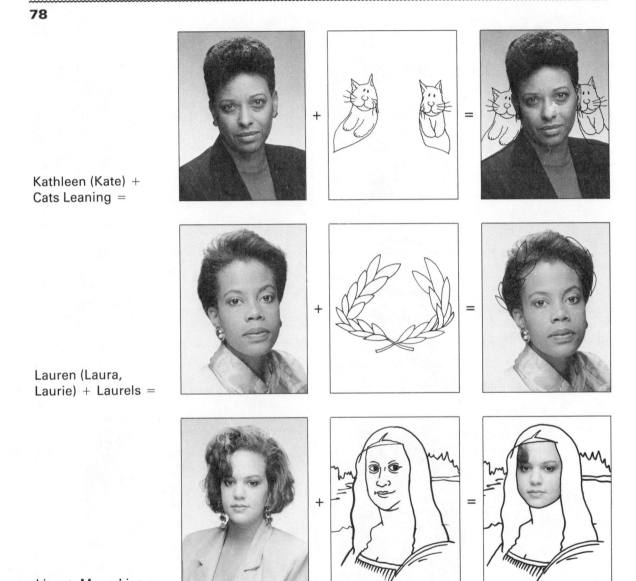

Kathleen (Kate) +
Cats Leaning =

Lauren (Laura,
Laurie) + Laurels =

Lisa + Mona Lisa =

Margaret (Marge) +
Margarine =

Marilyn +
Marilyn Monroe =

Mary + Mary "Had
a Little Lamb" =

Nancy (Nan) +
Nancy Reagan =

Patricia (Patty, Pat) +
Pat on the Head =

Ruth + Tooth =

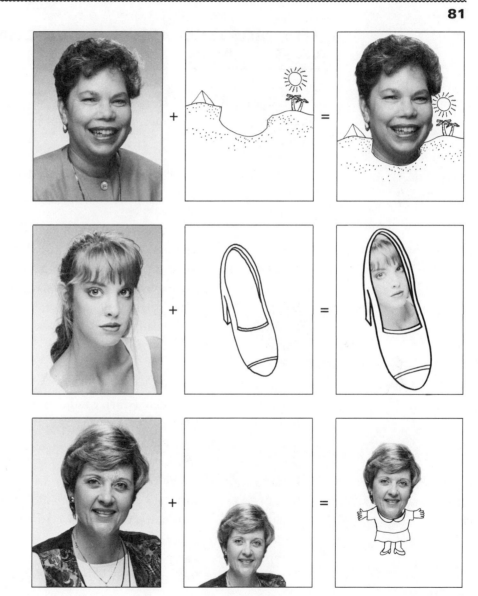

Sarah + Sahara =

Susan (Sue) + Shoe =

Tina + Tiny =

THE MOST COMMON AMERICAN LAST NAMES

The following is a list of 150 of the most common American last names, each accompanied by obvious cues that might help you fix these names in your memory.

Abbott	& Costello; a "butt" (cigarette butt)
Adams	Adam's apple
Allen	allen wrench
Anderson	Hans Christian Andersen character; Anderson window
Andrews	Andrews Air Force Base; hand drew
Bailey	bay leaves; Bailey's Irish Cream
Baker	baker's hat—rolling dough
Baldwin	bald (head) "1"; Baldwin organ
Barry	berry
Bell	bell
Bennett	bayonet
Bernstein	burn stain (scar), conductor's wand
Black	black color
Blake	lake, blink
Brooks	brook
Brown	brown color; Charlie Brown
Burke	burr
Burton	button, ton of burrs
Butler	butler
Campbell	Campbell's soup
Carson	Johnny Carson; Carson City; car & sun

Carter	Jimmy; Carter's children's wear; cart her
Clark	Clark candy bar
Cohen	cone
Collins	collie; Tom Collins drink
Cooper	chicken coop
Cunningham	sly ("cunning") ham; Ritchie Cunningham
Daniels	Jack Daniel's; lion's den; coonskin cap (Daniel Boone)
Davis	Bette Davis eyes
Donald	Donald Duck
Douglas	Douglas fir tree
Edwards	Edwards Air Force Base; King Edward (crown)
Ellis	Ellis Island
Evans	Bob Evans
Feinberg	fine (ticket); iceberg; bird
Feldman	felt on a man
Fisher	fisherman; fishing pole
Flanagan	Father Flanagan; "flan-again"
Foster	foster home; Foster's lager
Gardner	gardener
Gilbert	gills on Bert (from Sesame Street)
Ginsberg	gin on iceberg
Goodwin	good wind
Graham	graham cracker; grandma
Green	green color
Hall	hallway; Hall's cough drops
Hamilton	ham weighs a ton
Harper	harp player; *Harper's Bazaar*
Harris	hairless

Harrison	hairy son; hairy sun
Hartman	heart man; heart-shaped moon
Henderson	hen under son
Henry	hen on rye; hen with ray of sun
Hopkins	Johns Hopkins; kin hopping
Jackson	jacks with sun as the ball
Jacobs	Jacob's ladder
James	King James (crown); Jesse James
Jenkins	junk in
Johnson	john's son; Howard Johnson's; Johnson & Johnson
Jones	jeans
Jordan	Jordan River; country; Jordan almonds
Kaufman	cough man; man coughing
Keller	Helen Keller; killer; killer whale
Kennedy	JFK; RFK; can of dye; Kennedy Airport
King	crown; king piece from chess
Klein	climb; Calvin Klein
Kramer	creamer
Lang	long; laying
Larson	arson; larceny
Lawrence	Lawrence of Arabia; Lawrence Welk
Lee	leaf; lei
Levine	leaves on a vine
Levinson	leaving son; leaving sun
Levy	Levi's jeans
Lewis	St. Louis arch
McDonald	McDonald's golden arches; Duck (Donald)
Martin	martini
Maxwell	Maxwell House coffee

Meyer	admire; mayor; mare; my ear
Michaels	my calls; mike (microphone) kills
Miller	miller; Miller beer
Mitchell	shell in a mitt
Monroe	man rowing; Marilyn Monroe
Moore	mooring; more of
Morris	Morris the cat; more ice
Murphy	Murphy's oil soap; more fees
Nelson	wrestling hold
North	compass; North Pole
Oliver	olive
O'Neal	*O* kneel
Owens	owing; *O* wins
Palmer	palm tree; palm of hand
Patrick	hat trick; rich pats of butter
Patterson	pat her son
Paul	pallbearer; pull
Perkins	coffee percolating; Perkins restaurants
Perry	pears; pair of *E*'s
Peters	*P* tears
Philips	full lips; Phillips screwdriver; milk of magnesia; fill 'er up
Quinn	wind; queen
Randall	handle
Raymond	ray of sun on mount, mound
Reynolds	Reynolds Wrap
Richards	rich herds
Roberts	robbers
Robinson	robin's son

Rogers	Mr. Rogers; Rodgers & Hammerstein
Rosen	rose in vase
Rosenberg	rose in (ice) berg
Ross	Betsy Ross (flag)
Rubin	reuben sandwich
Russell	Jane Russell (full figures); rustling leaves; cattle rustling
Ryan	rye in (mouth)
Samuels	some mules
Schmidt	mitt (as in catcher's mitt)
Schneider	sniper; snide; cider
Schultz	Charles Schulz ("Peanuts")
Schwartz	warts; shorts
Scott	scotch, scot towels; Scot
Sears	Sears Roebuck
Sherman	sure man, shoreman; Sherman tank; the march
Simpson	Bart (cartoon character)
Sloan	loan; slow on
Smith	blacksmith
Spencer	suspenders
Stern	stern (of boat)
Steward	steward; hard stew
Sullivan	Ed Sullivan; sullied van
Swanson	swan son; swan song; Swanson's TV dinner
Tate	tight; Sharon Tate
Taylor	tailor
Thomas	tom-tom (on ass); mass of toes
Thompson	tom's son
Turner	Tina Turner; spatula (turner)

Tyler	tiler; tile her
Victor	winner; "V" victory sign
Wagner	wagon
Walker	baby walker; old person's walker
Wallace	wall of ice
Walters	wall of tears; Barbara Walters
Warner	warn her; Senator Warner
Watson	watt son, what son?; Doctor Watson
Webster	web stir; dictionary
Weiss	wise; ice
White	white color
Williams	will yams
Wilson	Wilson tennis balls; basketballs
Winston	Winston Churchill; Winston cigarettes
Wright	write; write
Young	baby; young person

7

The Final Exam

Now it's time to put some of your new skills into practice and to see how much you've improved in your ability to recall names and faces.

On the following pages we will have three trials, with nine names and faces in each. The tests are exactly like the ones you took in chapter 5.

Once again, you will need a pencil, and a watch with a minute hand. When you are ready to begin, you will study the faces on the next page for one minute. You will repeat the names out loud and use the techniques you picked up in the previous chapters. At the end of one minute, you will turn the page and fill in as many names as you can. If you're ready, you can begin.

FIRST TRY

Elizabeth

Norman

Henry

Christine

Mary

Raymond

Janice

James

Phyllis

IDENTIFY AS MANY AS YOU CAN

Please fill in as many names as you can on the opposite page. When you are finished, proceed to page 92.

SECOND TRY

Here are the same nine names and faces, only scrambled. Take another minute to study them. When you are finished, go to the following page and fill in as many names as you can.

Janice

Phyllis

Elizabeth

Raymond

Henry

Mary

Christine

Norman

James

IDENTIFY AS MANY AS YOU CAN

Please fill in as many names as you can on the opposite page. When you are finished, proceed to page 96.

_____

_____

_____

_____

_____

_____

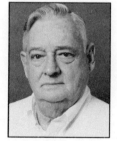

_____

_____

_____

THIRD TRY

For the last time, you see these nine names and faces, in yet a different arrangement. Take one minute to study them, then turn the page and fill in as many names as you can.

Christine

Raymond

James

Henry

Phyllis

Norman

Mary

Janice

Elizabeth

IDENTIFY AS MANY AS YOU CAN

This is the last trial. Please fill in as many names as you can, and proceed to the following page.

LAST NAMES QUIZ

Now you can try your hand at some last names. Here is a list of names that we provided cues for in the previous chapter. Use the blank space to fill in a cue or image that you would use to imprint the name in your memory.

Smith

Reynolds

Warner

Butler

Harrison

Maxwell

Abbott

Jacobs

Oliver

Bernstein

Green

Palmer

Quinn

Clark

Patterson

8

How to Remember
Just About Everything

A talk show host once asked me if there is such a thing as a "memory muscle"—that is, a part of your brain that can be strengthened with exercise. It was a good question, and a difficult one to answer.

Essentially, the more time you spend training your memory, the better your memory is going to be. If, for instance, you work hard at improving your ability to recall names and faces, very likely this will also help you remember where you put your glasses—simply because you are going to be more attentive to your actions and your environment in general.

While this book focuses primarily on remembering people's names, there are a lot of minutiae in daily life that must be taken in, stored, and retrieved. This chapter will discuss some of the best techniques for remembering such things as phone numbers, addresses, and lists, as well as where you put misplaced objects. You will also learn how to retain information and how to recall that information when you need it.

First, however, let's discuss some rather simple techniques that will further reinforce your ability to remember people's names.

TAKING THE NAME-FACE ASSOCIATION PERSONALLY

In earlier chapters, you learned what our researchers found to be the most effective technique for remembering people's names and faces. But there are some things you can do to *personalize* the technique and make it work even better for you. If some of the following techniques seem to fall under the "commonsense" heading, all the better.

• *Listen carefully to the person's name when you are introduced.* Ask the person to repeat the name if you do not hear it clearly. This will rarely offend anyone and your interest will often please the other person.

• *Repeat the person's name when you are introduced and once or twice afterward if you are involved in conversation.*

• *Look at the person and try to form a clear picture of him or her in your mind.* Use the name-face association technique at this point, or simply repeat the person's name while holding the image you have formed in your mind.

• *After the initial meeting with someone, take the opportunity to write down his or her name.* If you used the name-face association technique, note the distinguished feature you used or other information that might be helpful later.

• *If you fail to recall someone's name, don't panic.* The other person is probably having just as much difficulty remembering your name!

• *Don't try to remember too many names at once.* Decide who is important to meet and know before you attend an event or participate in a meeting. If you are under forty, a reasonable goal is to remember three names. If you are between forty and sixty, try two names at first. If you are over sixty, one name is good for starters. If you need to, you can work up to higher numbers from there, but remember, the point is not to make this into a memory marathon, but to heighten your efficiency at personal relations.

• *Go for the obvious.* If you meet someone who is named Shirley—and you have an Aunt Shirley—no need to stretch for a Shirley MacLaine or Shirley Temple. Think about how she does—or doesn't—look like your Aunt Shirley, and you will be way ahead of the game.

• *Silliness can be a great help.* To remember first and last names, don't wring your hands over Steven Peters. Make it Steve Pete. Or, instead of Sharon Williams, plug Sharon Bill into your memory. Amusing or even ridiculous shortcuts are wonderfully effective.

• *Remember the people in the order in which you've met them.* This is a version of the method of loci, and it helps immensely. If you walk into a conference room, start around the table—much as a waiter might —and fix each name and face into your memory, *in order.* It gives you another way to track the names and faces visually.

• *Sort out the names and faces as they are introduced.* Don't over-burden yourself with names and faces you don't really need to know. Sometimes remembering a face can be enough. But if you meet someone whom you know you'll never see or hear of again, don't bother to mem-orize his or her name; it's just not worth it.

• *If it is an uncommon name, ask about it.* Many foreign names are hard to grasp in the first go-around, and asking about the origin of the name or even how to spell it is fair play.

As we discussed before, remembering a person's name is probably the most appreciated courtesy one can extend to another. Once you strengthen your own abilities to remember people's names, there is a kind of graduate level of courtesy you can aspire to, which is helping *other* people remember people's names. It is an act of consideration, to be sure, but it also will help your own efforts to secure a name.

• Be certain that the focus of the attention is on the introduction. If people are engaging in small talk, wait until it is over, then make the introduction.

• When several introductions are to be made, pause between each one of them.

• If possible, repeat the name: "Mary, this is Bob. Bob is director of marketing for ABC Corporation. Bob, Mary will be involved in the selection of the convention site, which we'll be discussing later."

• During the ensuing interaction—be it a dinner party or a business conference—repeat the individual names as often as seems appropriate. Instead of simply turning to someone and saying "That's an interesting point," say "That's an interesting point, Gary."

• If you are trying to help someone remember *your* name, accent the name portion, either with timing, tone of voice, or pitch. Also, if it is appropriate, repeat your first name: "Hello. I'm John Baker, but please call me John."

HOW TO REMEMBER WHERE
YOU PUT YOUR GLASSES

(KEYS, WEDDING RING, WALLET, AND
JUST ABOUT EVERYTHING ELSE)

If you're forgetful, misplaced items can be the bane of your existence. Moreover, you will not be spared this annoyance until you make a commitment to become more aware of your behavior as it relates to your ability to remember where you just put something.

The first thing to appreciate about objects like keys and glasses is that they are so easy to misplace because you put them in literally hundreds of different places during your lifetime, thus creating hundreds of opportunities for forgetfulness.

The obvious strategy for keys is to determine once and for all a place to put them, every time, no matter what. A drawer. A peg. A position on the kitchen counter. A special little box or bowl. Have a family meeting and announce that the placement of the keys in this spot is mandatory and punishable by . . . whatever. Your problem, I guarantee, will be over.

The problem with misplaced glasses and wedding rings is a little more complex. You take your glasses off at different times for different reasons, and it is impractical to think that you would scurry downstairs to a prescribed place—the kitchen counter, for instance—after finishing a novel in bed. In situations like this, the use of a sensory technique works very well. Again, as you may recall from previous chapters, the solution lies in dramatizing the otherwise undramatic.

The goal is to make the ordinary become extraordinary. In the case of your glasses, for instance, you will want to dramatize where you place them, each time you put them down. Say you place them on your nightstand, near the alarm clock. Mentally imagine the alarm clock ringing loudly as you put them down. If you put them in your purse, imagine your purse coming alive and gobbling up the glasses. Again, the more theatrical or absurd you can make the dramatization, the better your chances of remembering where you put something.

Here are some other suggestions for improving your loss-find ratio, especially when it comes to household items.

• When you misplace an object or forget what you were after when you enter a room, mentally retrace your steps. If this doesn't work, *physically* retrace your steps. For example, you are brushing your teeth and suddenly recall that you need to bring something to work that is located in your den. You go to the den, but when you get there, you draw a blank. In this case you should go back to the bathroom and literally pick up your toothbrush—re-creating the scene as best you can—and you will probably remember the item in question.

• If you commonly misplace a certain item, use your own voice to reinforce your memory. Say out loud, "I am placing my camera on the black bookcase." This may seem odd to family members, but that's a small price to pay. You will improve your recall *significantly*.

• When you go into a room to get something, mentally enlarge the item and position it in an unusual spot in the room. For example, suppose you are going into the living room to get the latest issue of a certain magazine. As you walk from the kitchen to the living room, picture an enormous version of the magazine reclining on the couch. Most likely you will not forget what you were looking for, even if you are interrupted along the way.

• You may have trouble misplacing large objects, such as your car! The answer here is obvious, to help remember where you park your car while shopping or going to a sporting event, place an unusual flag on your antenna.

• Another cue for recalling the location of your car: try to always park in the same spot or area. For example, if you regularly shop at a mall, always park by the same department store.

REMEMBERING LISTS OF ALL KINDS

The obvious strategy for remembering a list is to write it down, and then not to lose the paper it's written on. To help with the latter problem, one person I know always wads up a piece of paper before putting it into his pocket so as to create an obvious bulge.

For most of us, though, we have neither the time nor the inclination to write a list for everything we need to remember. For these situations, the strategy I recommend was briefly described in chapter 3 on page 32, the link-chain technique.

Here's how it works. Suppose you have to make a stop at the grocery on your way home from work. You are mulling over what you need for tonight's dinner and for the household, and you come up with this: flounder, flour, tea bags, lemon, dishwasher detergent. What you want to do is employ as many senses as you can so that the list is more memorable. So you animate the list: The flounder is swimming through a bag of flour and making a mess. The fish flops onto a box of tea bags and it rains lemon juice, somewhat cleaning the fish. Then dishwasher detergent is applied for good measure.

Ludicrous? Certainly. But that's the point. This kind of imagery can stay with you for days, and it really works.

There are other, similar techniques you can apply to remembering lists. Here are a few:

• Create a fictional character who can be easily visualized. Whenever you think of something you need to get done, picture the character performing the task. If this is difficult for you, picture yourself completing all of the tasks you need to complete, in order.

• To remember a grocery list, compose it aisle by aisle. By applying an order to the list, you will make it more memorable.

• To remember a list of items that you want to pack for a trip, go through your daily routine mentally ("First I wash my face, then brush my hair, then put on makeup") to pack your health and beauty aids. For your clothes, take it day by day ("What will I wear to the meetings all day? What will I wear that evening?" and so on).

THE NUMBERS GAME

REMEMBERING ZIPS, PHONE NUMBERS, AND ADDRESSES

Most of us don't have to remember numbers on a daily basis, but there are times when it makes life so much easier to have that phone number memorized for instant recall.

For instance, when I made the arrangements to write this book—and knew that I would be calling my agent and coauthor on a regular basis—I made the decision to memorize their two new phone numbers just to make life easier. By the same token, when a dear friend or a relative moves and you know you'll be writing to that person frequently, why not memorize the address and zip code? Why have to look it up all the time?

If you find yourself wanting or needing to remember a number, again, apply the guiding principle: *Make it meaningful.* Your sister's new phone number is 725-4192. How would you break apart that number? You could use dates: 725 could be July 25. You could use years: 41 is the year Pearl Harbor was bombed, 92 is the current year. You could use ages: 725 might become 7, the age of your niece; and 25, the age you were when you got married. All of these and many more variations can be applied, no matter what kind of number you are trying to remember.

The other technique to use when you are memorizing numbers is chunking. We talked about it in chapter 1, when we discussed how short- and long-term memory work. Basically, it means that you can group or cluster numbers into as many as seven chunks to make the process more manageable. A telephone number like (212) 725-4192 could be viewed as three chunks or could be broken down another way: (212) 7-25-41-92 could be viewed as five chunks. Your mind will do this somewhat naturally for you, but if you consciously use chunking as a tool, you will be all the better off.

SOME REMINDERS

Half of the battle of remembering things on a daily basis is setting up a system of reminders for yourself, ranging from putting it off on your spouse ("Remind me to pick up Billy's bike from the repair shop, honey") to tying a string around your finger.

Here is a small collection of tips to help you remember whatever it is you need to remember:

• Don't laugh at the standard string around the finger. Anything odd or out of place can help trigger your memory. A watch worn on the wrong wrist or a crumpled dollar bill in your change purse can serve as a signal, and the clearer you make the association (the crumpled bill could serve to remind you that you need to make a trip to the bank), the better.

• Expanding on the "out of place" concept, intentionally leave objects out of place to remember a task that is related to the object. For example, leave your dry cleaning slip on the seat of your car or leave your watering can in the middle of the kitchen to help you remember about the cleaning or watering the plants.

• You can also use physical reminders that are not necessarily out of place. For instance, you could leave letters you need to mail with your car keys.

• If you are one of those people who remembers to bring the letters with you but forgets to mail them, use associative cues. For instance, you could picture the letters flying toward the mailbox, or picture the person you are writing to sitting on top of the mailbox or reading your letter.

• When making appointments—such as a doctor's appointment or a dentist's appointment—try to schedule it at the same time of day each time and, if possible, on the same day of the week.

• If you have a difficulty remembering what you were doing before you were interrupted, leave yourself a cue. Say you are reading a magazine article and the phone rings: mark where you were with a pen and bring the article with you to the phone.

• Bring along physical cues that will remind you of errands or tasks you need to perform. For example, bring the empty pill bottle for your prescription in your purse or your pocket to remind yourself to get a refill. Or bring along to the office an invitation that needs an RSVP.

• Did you remember to turn off the coffeepot? Many people drive themselves crazy worrying about such things as whether they locked the garage door or unplugged the iron. Develop your own checklist system for leaving the house. A written checklist would be great, but in lieu of that a mental walk-through the house will help you remember what you need to do before you're halfway across town.

HOW TO REMEMBER WHAT YOU JUST READ

There is a final category of forgetfulness that deserves at least a quick mention, and it falls under the general heading of "retention." The need to absorb and retain information does not end when we graduate from formal academic study. Most people continue to learn and amass information throughout their lifetimes.

Research suggests that the most effective way to take in a large amount of material is to break it down in small, manageable sections. Not only does this give your mind a chance to make connections and absorb the material, but the simple act of taking a break and giving the mind a rest enhances retention.

For really weighty material, I suggest the following:

• Before you read it, skim it. Read the headings, look at the graphs or illustrations, get a sense of the material.

• Based on your survey, formulate some questions about the material you are about to read. If there are questions at the end of the chapter, read through them before you start reading the text.

• Read the text.

• If appropriate, go back and highlight or underline the important sections.

• Review the text.

THE FORGETFUL PERSON'S SHOPPING LIST

The marketplace is full of notebooks and pads and gadgets designed to help you remember things more easily, and here is a selective shopping list that could make your life easier.

• If you tend to burn pots and pans and often forget that you've got something cooking on the stove, buy an old-fashioned timer. They are available at variety stores and sell for under $10.

• As the famous psychologist B. F. Skinner wrote, "Rely on memoranda, not on memory." The little yellow or blue Post-It notes are invaluable reminders: plaster them on cabinets, doors, the telephone—wherever you need to make an impact.

• Is this obvious? Buy an appointment book. Whether you work in an office or at home or are retired, you need a running log of things you need to do.

• Go to the hardware store and have a few extra sets of keys made. Be sure to test all of them. Then put one set in a secure outdoor location today. (Don't forget where you put it.)

• Buy a slew of notepads and put them in the following locations: bedside table, kitchen near the phone, and in the car.

• Leave messages to yourself on your answering machine. If you are out of your home and think of a task you must complete later in the day or evening, don't rely on your memory—call and leave *yourself* a message.

• If you must remember to do something in an hour, or two hours, set an alarm or automatic timer to go off at the appropriate time. Chances are, when the buzzer sounds, you'll remember to complete the task.

9

Memory Fitness
for Fun

Practice, in memory training, doesn't guarantee perfection—but it does help you develop some good habits, particularly through playing memory games that help you to sharpen your attentiveness. What follows is a series of exercises that you can do whenever you want and as many times as you want. I recommend you try three or four in the next few days just to see if your mind begins to focus more tightly on the people, places, and things around you.

☞ Before you sit down to read a magazine or newspaper article, tell yourself that you will be asked to summarize its contents for someone. Be aware of how differently you approach the material, and of the associations your mind naturally makes. Also, practice finding the topic sentence in each sentence or paragraph. Make up your own headline for different sections of the article or essay.

☞ Every week you probably take the same route to such places as the grocer, the dry cleaners, and the office. This week stop and notice new landmarks along the routes. Pay attention to the street names, as if you will be required to give directions to someone later. This will help you develop a more active sense of awareness.

☞ Make better use of "wasted" time. While you are in the shower, for instance, make a mental list of the things you have to do that day and associate some part of your bathing ritual with something that needs to be done. For example, if you need to book an airline reservation, think of it while washing the "wings" on your back; if you need to order some computer paper, imagine the paper with shampoo all over it.

☞ To help you get in the habit of remembering lists of all kinds, practice with food items. Make a meal out of the items, even if it doesn't make sense. If the list is soup, celery, strawberries, chicken, oranges, potato chips, salad dressing, and milk, imagine a meal made of cream of chicken soup made with milk and celery, potato chips with dressing, and strawberry-orange salad for dessert. Practice with your real grocery lists.

☞ Practice creating acronyms for the items on your shopping or "to do" lists. For example, pick up *dry* cleaning, drop off party *invitations*, call in *prescription* refill, and *shop* for groceries might be DIPS.

☞ Remembering license plate numbers is an excellent game to play and there are several ways to go about it. For instance, try converting the initials to a semi-meaningful word: VKG might be *viking* or FML might be *formal*. Just do the letters at first. Numbers will come later.

The next time, try converting the numbers to dates or numeric sequences. For dates, 0534 could be May 34; 8621 becomes August 6, 1921. Or, to use numeric sequences beginning with 2, 238 becomes 2 to the third power equals 8. You can also combine the two techniques like this: 468-0534 would be an even-number sequence beginning with 4, followed by May 34.

☞ Next time you are on the bus or subway or waiting in line, study the faces around you. Half the challenge of name-face association is becoming better attuned to facial features. Practice exaggerating features and studying facial composition, hair, skin, and other distinctive aspects of facial appearance.

☞ Another great venue for practicing name-face association is television. Programs like "The MacNeil-Lehrer NewsHour" and even the afternoon talk shows feature a lot of guests whose faces and names you can study.

☞ Another exercise you can perform to increase awareness is to walk into a room and mentally note where ten objects in the room are placed. Once you leave the room, try to picture where each of the ten items is. Do this each day, with different objects in different rooms, until you are able to accurately recall all ten objects.

☞ There is a technique cumbersomely called the substitution-transformation technique that can be used for remembering the names of places by creating absurd imagery. A restaurant called the Snuggery might conjure up some food item wrapped up, snug in a rug. Practice this technique as you drive down the road—for restaurants, stores, gas stations, or whatever else you find.

☞ Each day decide that you will remember a certain thought at a certain time. For instance, decide you will call your mother at eight P.M., or that you will think of a favorite quotation at five P.M. Try not to think about it again until the appointed time. It is important to note at the end of each day how you did and to make a new resolution for the next day. This will take some time (perhaps as long as a month), but do this every day until you have mastered this ability. It will give you an extraordinary confidence in your memory.

☞ Memorize items or statistics that are of interest to you. It can be anything: the names of the actors and actresses on your favorite television show, current records of local sports teams—even (and this is especially good) poetry or quotes by thinkers you respect. Memorizing is a lost and important art, and aids memory training, in general, enormously.

☞ The next time you attend a party, make a point of remembering four names. Increase that number to five, then six or more. Reinforce the names several times during the event by talking to yourself ("The woman talking to my wife is Brenda"). Check your performance at the end of the event.

☞ Memorize numbers that are a part of your life but that currently you may not pay much attention to—your credit card numbers, for instance. Also your spouse's or children's Social Security numbers or the phone numbers of the dry cleaners, the butcher, or other services you use every now and then.

☞ Practice recalling your lists as you write them. After completing a list, turn it over and try to recall as many items as you can. Check your performance by reviewing the list again. Even if you remember only half of the items on the list, you will have better placed those items in your memory.

☞ Think up your own ROY-G-BIV and "Every Good Boy Does Fine" cues.

☞ Practice focusing on a specific facial feature each week. For instance, one week focus on the appearance of people's eyes; the next week look at nothing but noses.

☞ Look up the phone numbers of your three favorite restaurants and commit them to memory using the technique for memorizing numbers in the previous chapter. Once you have committed them to memory, reward yourself by calling for reservations.

☞ Practice using all of your senses. When you order a dish at a restaurant, note the texture, the subtle flavorings, the temperature, and the colors. When you see a flower arrangement, note the different types and shapes of flowers, the smells and colors, and the type of vase. When you are shopping for an item of clothing, feel the textures, note the different shades of colors, the garment's lines, and, of course, the price.

☞ Memorize recipes for food and drinks by visualizing the process of preparing the recipe, using as many senses as you can.

☞ The next time you go to a party, be aware of what you find naturally engaging and interesting. You will find some patterns will emerge. A husband and wife can chat with someone and come away with a totally different set of impressions and details, depending on their own interests and motivations. By the end of the evening you will see how attentive you are to *certain* things without even trying.

☞ Are you a Type A personality, or Type B? Type A's, as they are sometimes described, are people who need to feel that they are in control; they are often perfectionists, bent on achievement and very goal-oriented. Type B's, by contrast, are less rigid and more conceptual. They achieve no less than the Type A, but they go about it without the need to set constant goals.

If you are a Type A, you need to set realistic goals for yourself in memory training. Don't go overboard. Let the techniques settle in and avoid the temptation to move too quickly through the process. Don't try to do all of the exercises in this chapter *this week*. Spread them out over a period of time.

If you are a Type B, you probably will need to become more goal-oriented about your memory training. In this case, the exercises furnished here should be of immense value to you because they offer a structured means of practicing memory techniques. Commit yourself to at least two exercises a week.

☞ The next time you walk into a business meeting, decide whose names you need to remember beforehand and limit your efforts to those people alone.

☞ Select someone you have dealt with for years but still don't call by name: your butcher, your gas attendant, your dry cleaner. Ask for his or her name and begin to use it every now and then. Watch for the Dale Carnegie effect.